DRAW! CARS

BY **Doug DuBosque**

Scholastic Inc.
New York Toronto London Auckland Sydney

For Rick, who taught me, at a tender age,
everything there was to know about his
Triumph TR4...except how to use the clutch.

ISBN 0-590-11746-7

12 11 10 9 8 7 6 5 4 3 2   7 8 9/9 0 1 2/0

Printed in the U.S.A.   34
First Scholastic printing, September 1997

CONTENTS

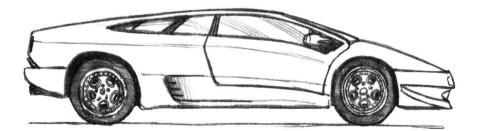

WHAT YOU NEED

You can draw with just about anything. (After all, people in caves used dried clay and black stuff out of the fire pit, and we're still talking about their drawings 25,000 years later!)

To get good at drawing (which means, to have the most fun with it) you need a comfortable place to draw — make sure there's decent light, so you can see what you're doing. Figure out a way to store your drawings — you'll find instructions for a simple portfolio on page 80. Keep your drawings, even not-so-good ones, and learn from them.

I suggest you start out lightly in pencil, so you can erase problems as you need to. You can't do that with a marker! Remember that you won't become an expert overnight — but as you practice, you'll get better, and you'll enjoy watching your own improvement!

Pencil—longer than your finger, please

Eraser—not the one on your pencil, which will disappear quickly

Paper—I use "junk" paper to practice—backs of old photocopies and computer printouts work well, and the price is right!

Pencil sharpener

Ruler or straightedge—but you won't need it often

POSITIVE ATTITUDE:
DO YOUR BEST!

DRAW! CARS

FROM THE SIDE

This is a basic introduction to drawing a car from the side. You'll start out with boxes and circles, which you'll draw very lightly. Then you'll change the shapes and add details, a little bit at a time, until you have a finished drawing of a car.

You'll find several pages devoted to just wheels, since they're one of the hardest parts to draw.

After that, you'll find a collection of different cars and other vehicles from the side. Some have photos; all but one have in-between drawings, to show you how to get from the basic boxes to a finished drawing you'll be happy to show off.

Watch for ★ **Technique Tips.** These can help save you a lot of time!

Step 1: Here's the beginning of our car drawing. Draw a line for the ground. After all, cars spend most of their time on the ground.

The ground.

Step 2: Next, add a circle for a wheel.

Step 3: Figure out where the second wheel goes.

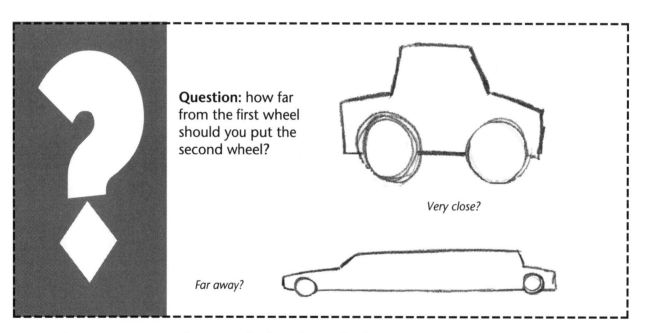

Question: how far from the first wheel should you put the second wheel?

Very close?

Far away?

The general rule is three wheels, more or less.

Answer: three wheels, more or less.

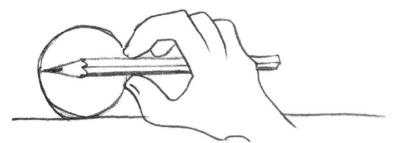

Here's how to draw it.

1) See above: use your pencil to measure how wide the wheel is. (Put the pencil point on one side of the wheel, and use your thumb and finger to mark the other side of the wheel.)

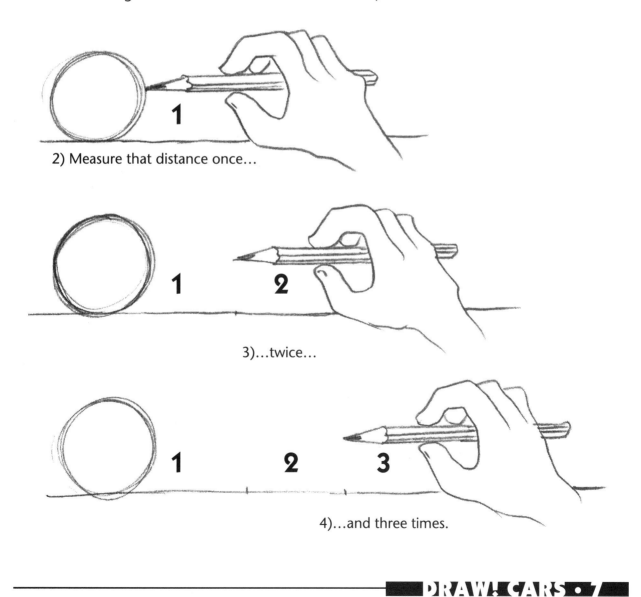

2) Measure that distance once…

3) …twice…

4) …and three times.

Step 4: Now add the second wheel. You can see that almost three wheels could fit between it and the first wheel. Not all cars are the same, so always measure the wheels before you draw.

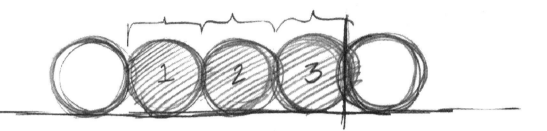

Step 5: Draw a box. Draw it very lightly, so you can erase part of it later. The bottom of the box is below the center of the wheels. The top of the box is not as high as you might think. The ends of the box stick out beyond the wheels at both ends.

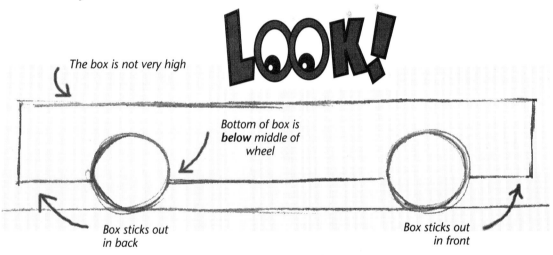

The box is not very high

LOOK!

*Bottom of box is **below** middle of wheel*

Box sticks out in back

Box sticks out in front

When you look at a real car, you can use this same measuring technique. For best results, hold your pencil at arm's length and look with one eye closed.

Step 6:

Add a second box, on top of the first box. Start it at the back end of the bottom box, but make it shorter than the first box, and also not as high. See where mine ends, at the back of the front wheel?

★ **Technique Tip:** draw these boxes *very lightly...!*

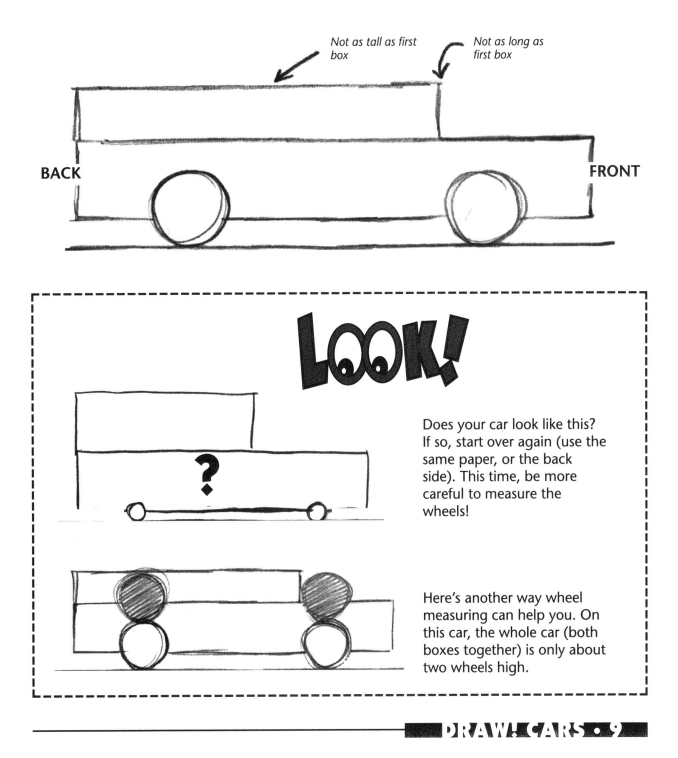

Not as tall as first box

Not as long as first box

BACK

FRONT

LOOK!

?

Does your car look like this? If so, start over again (use the same paper, or the back side). This time, be more careful to measure the wheels!

Here's another way wheel measuring can help you. On this car, the whole car (both boxes together) is only about two wheels high.

Step 7: Make the front slope downward a little bit. This is a small, but important, change! Notice: the front of the car does NOT come to a point!

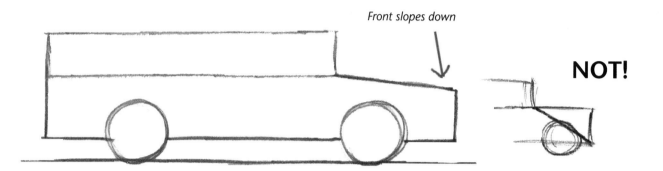

Front slopes down

NOT!

Step 8: Next, slope the windshield. The sloped windshield helps the car's aerodynamics. This means it slides through the air more easily. People who design cars use wind tunnels and computers to test their designs. If a car slides through the air more easily, it can use less fuel.

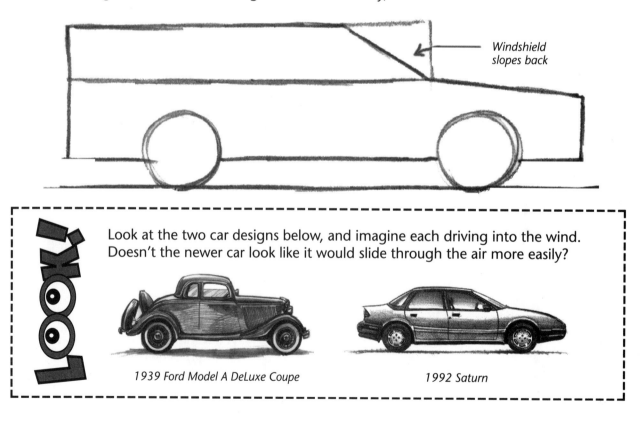

Windshield slopes back

Look at the two car designs below, and imagine each driving into the wind. Doesn't the newer car look like it would slide through the air more easily?

1939 Ford Model A DeLuxe Coupe

1992 Saturn

What next? With two boxes, you can create just about any kind of vehicle. For example, here's how you could make a four-wheel-drive vehicle:

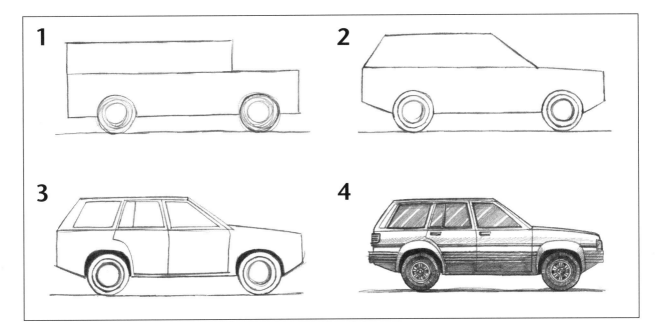

You can also make a convertible… can you see how? (You don't even need the top box!)

OR you can draw a pickup truck.

There's no magic here. Once you understand the basics, you can use this technique on your own — and draw real-looking cars, from photographs or by looking at actual cars.

Step 9: Slope the back window downward. Very important: notice where it lines up with the back wheel!

Back window slopes

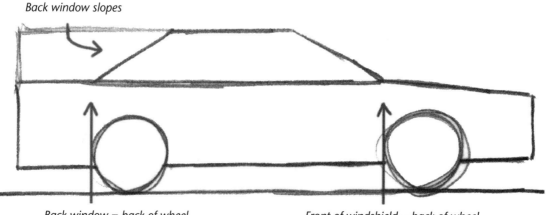

Back window = back of wheel   *Front of windshield = back of wheel*

On almost every car, the passenger compartment extends over the back wheel, but not over the front wheel. You'll see this even on very old cars.

1946 Chrysler Town & Country Four-Door Sedan

Step 10: On newer cars, often the whole car slopes down toward the front. Make the back of the car a little bit higher than the front.

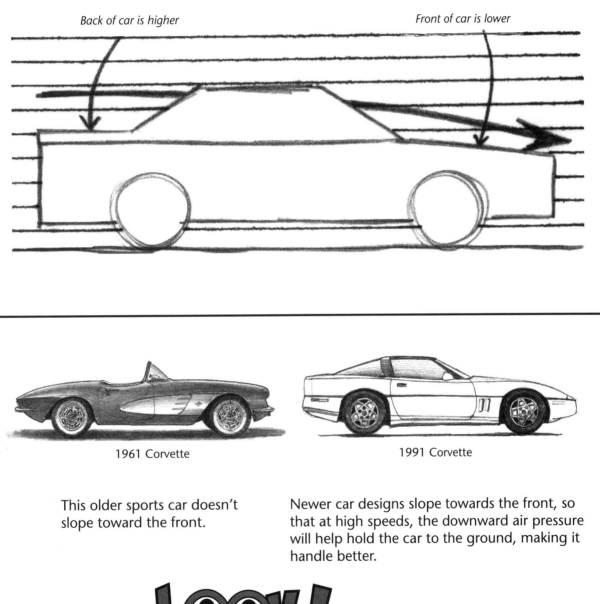

Back of car is higher

Front of car is lower

1961 Corvette

1991 Corvette

This older sports car doesn't slope toward the front.

Newer car designs slope towards the front, so that at high speeds, the downward air pressure will help hold the car to the ground, making it handle better.

Step 11: Add wheel wells. Wheel wells are the space above the tires. This space keeps the tires from hitting the body of the car when the car goes over bumps. Draw a line along the side of the car: many cars have one, and it's important to include it in your drawing. Also, on this car, you'll see a line around each fender. Add those lines, too.

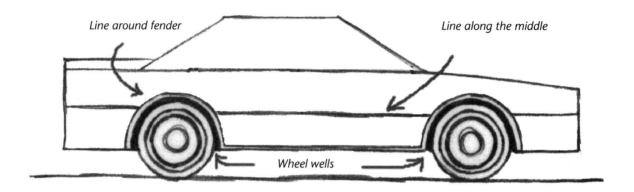

Line around fender   Line along the middle

Wheel wells

Now add doors and windows. If your car has four doors, you'll see two on each side — usually the back door circles around the rear wheel well.

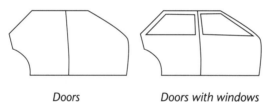

Doors   Doors with windows

First, draw a line down the middle to divide the two doors, then add the other lines. If you're not sure where to put the line, try measuring from the wheels, as you did earlier.

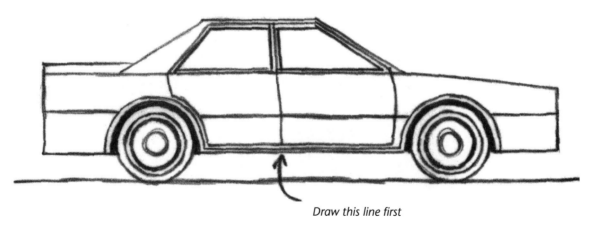

Draw this line first

Step 12: Finish the drawing. Add details, like lights, bumpers, antenna (or antennae, if you want more than one), and wheel designs (see the next few pages for ideas). Erase any boxy lines that still show (you did draw them lightly, didn't you?). Add shading or color if you want. Try drawing straight lines, or streaks, on the glass to make it look more real.

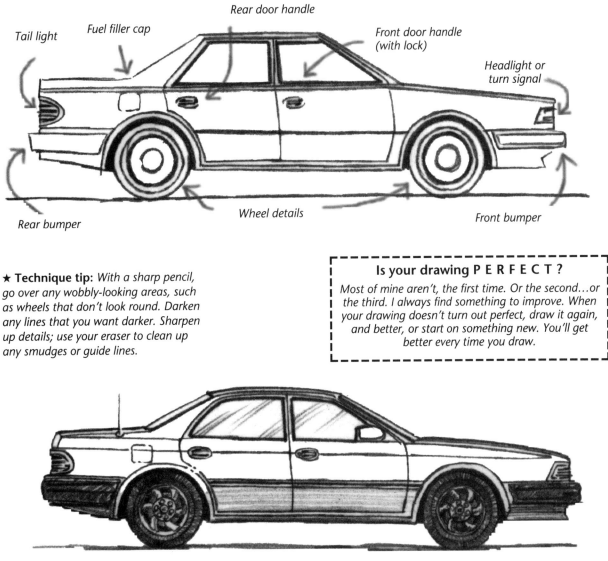

Rear door handle

Fuel filler cap

Tail light

Front door handle (with lock)

Headlight or turn signal

Rear bumper

Wheel details

Front bumper

★ **Technique tip:** *With a sharp pencil, go over any wobbly-looking areas, such as wheels that don't look round. Darken any lines that you want darker. Sharpen up details; use your eraser to clean up any smudges or guide lines.*

Is your drawing P E R F E C T ?
Most of mine aren't, the first time. Or the second...or the third. I always find something to improve. When your drawing doesn't turn out perfect, draw it again, and better, or start on something new. You'll get better every time you draw.

1992 Mitsubishi Diamante

➡ ➡ ➡ NEXT: want to have some WHEEL fun? ➡ ➡ ➡

Question: What's the difference between a wheel and a tire?

Answer: the wheel is the metal part in the middle. The tire is the rubber part on the outside.

Wheels and tires come in different sizes.

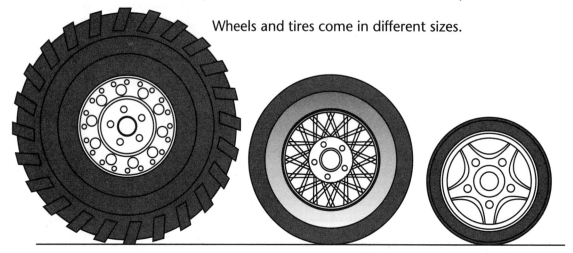

In this diagram, the *wheels* are the same size—but the tires sure aren't!

Not sure the wheels are really the same size? Compare them. Try measuring with your pencil.

HOW DO YOU MAKE WHEELS ROUND?

Guess what? Drawing wheels isn't easy!

For perfectly round wheels, you could use a computer drawing program to generate perfect circles. Or…

…you could purchase a template, used for technical drawing, which has round holes of different sizes. You carefully draw two perpendicular lines, and use them to line up the template for whatever size circle you want. It's not as easy at it looks! Or…

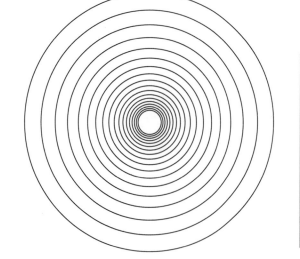

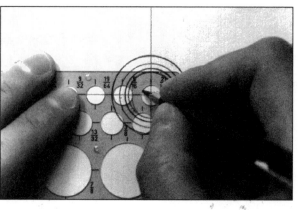

How Do You Make Wheels Round (CONTINUED)?

...or, with a compass, you can draw a circle, and you can also divide your circle into six parts for a great looking wheel. However, not many real car wheels have six-part designs!

After you draw the circle, mark one point on its circumference....

Starting with that point, mark off all the way around the circle with the compass...and you'll divide it into six parts.

To draw wheels, you must really *look* at wheels — you'll be amazed how many different designs there are! Sometimes, you'll find a wheel with no spokes or holes, but that's unusual.

Some designs are based on three, or four — but they're also unusual.

Some of the most expensive cars have wheels with designs based on five...

Lamborghini Countache

Lamborghini Diablo

Porsche 911

Ferrari Testarossa

...and in fact, you'll see many designs based on five, with curved or angled lines. Five-part designs just seem to be attractive to a lot of people.

Each part of a five-part design can be divided in two, giving you a ten-part design — or divided in three, giving you a fifteen-part design, or even a twenty-part design. *Count them and see for yourself!*

How many?

How many?

1970's Lamborghini

Mercedes Benz

These wheels are based on six — which, when divided, makes a12-part design *Count them for yourself!*

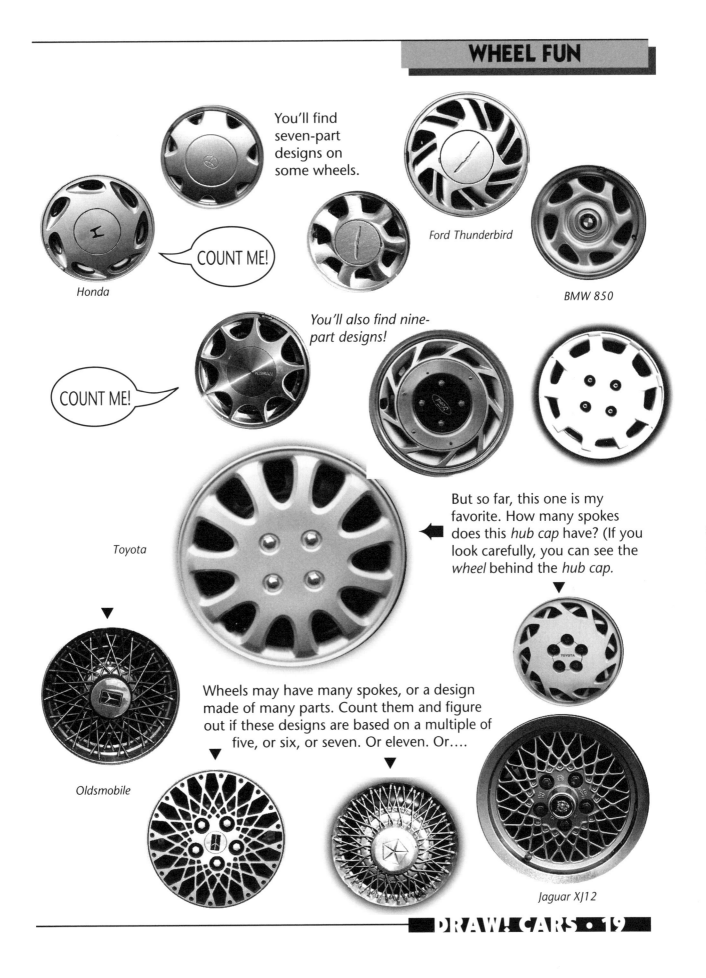

You'll find seven-part designs on some wheels.

COUNT ME!

Honda

Ford Thunderbird

BMW 850

You'll also find nine-part designs!

COUNT ME!

But so far, this one is my favorite. How many spokes does this *hub cap* have? (If you look carefully, you can see the *wheel* behind the *hub cap*.

Toyota

Oldsmobile

Wheels may have many spokes, or a design made of many parts. Count them and figure out if these designs are based on a multiple of five, or six, or seven. Or eleven. Or....

Jaguar XJ12

INVENT YOUR OWN WHEELS!

WHEELS NEED TO BE ROUND

OR THEY WON'T ROLL...

The most fun wheels are the ones you invent — after all, your drawing is *your* drawing! You can make the wheels, or the car, anyway you like. So experiment! Have fun! *Break the rules!*

Ooops…Wait a minute. There is one rule you probably shouldn't break. That rule is: **Wheels need to be round, or else they're not wheels!** *Draw those circles carefully!*

Dude!

While you're at it, feel free to experiment with the *size* of the wheels, too!

★ **Technique Tip:** To draw really round wheels, learn to turn your paper as you work, and draw only the part that fits the natural curve of your drawing hand. Place a piece of scrap paper under your hand as you draw so you won't smudge other parts of your drawing.

DRAW! CARS

SOME FAVORITES, FROM THE SIDE

*In this section, we'll take the two-box approach, and apply it to some favorites. I've included photographs whenever possible. This is to remind you of the importance of **reference material**.*

You don't just make it all up in your head — if you want to draw a real-looking car, you have to know what it looks like, which means looking at the car, or at a photograph of it!

*But don't stop with just a real-looking car. Once you've got the basics down, use your imagination! If you want smoke and flames or your own name on the side of the car — do it! After all, it's **your** drawing. Make it unique!*

__Technical note:__ when you take a photo of a car from the side, perspective creeps in — sometimes you see all four tires. In some of the drawings that follow, I've corrected perspective to make the drawing a true profile (and easier to draw).

LAMBORGHINI DIABLO

This is the newest, and hottest, car from Lamborghini, a company that started out making tractors, but became widely known for its supercars.

The top box is very low on this car!

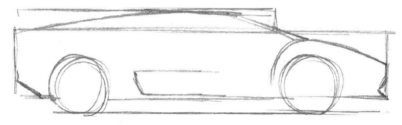

On a car like this, the boxes don't really look like much, but they can help you see proportions. Draw very carefully — *and lightly* — at first. Pay special attention to angles.

Exotic cars don't have much luggage space. So remember: when you set out to travel somewhere in a car like this, don't plan to take a lot of stuff with you!

Diablo wheel

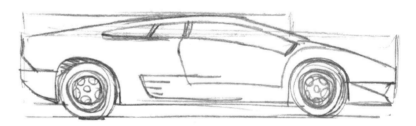

Measure the wheels! This car is *less than two wheels high*. The engine is behind the driver, and very large, which is why the door is so far forward. *Take your time drawing the wheels — they can make or break your drawing.*

LAMBORGHINI COUNTACHE

Again, the top box is *very* low.

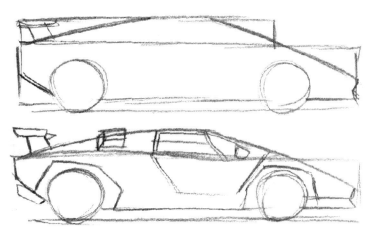

This outrageous-looking car had a little problem at first. The air scoops above the rear wheels had to be added because the engine overheated.

(That didn't stop just about everybody from thinking it was just about the coolest thing on wheels.)

The front comes almost to a point. Look at how the back goes up from the rear wheel.

For the rest of the details on the car, look at your *reference material* — either my photo, above, or a photo from somewhere else. My photo was taken with a wide-angle lens…can you see the *distortion*? Look carefully at the photo — you'll see that the rear wheel in the photo is not actually round.

FERRARI F40

This was the fortieth anniversary special from Ferrari, a company whose cars have won many races.

The F40 is basically a racing car modified for street use. Only 1,000 or so were produced (Ferrari keeps the exact number a secret). As of 1993, the average F40 (used) costs over $400,000.

(Will that be cash or charge?)

Use the boxes I showed you any way they work best. This whole car seems to slant forward, so my bottom box has a slanted top — but the bottom is level to the ground.

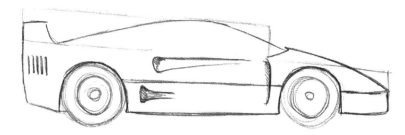

If you didn't look carefully, you might think the front of the F40 comes to a point — but look again.

When someone looks at your drawing, they won't notice all the mistakes that you see and think are absolutely horrible. So relax; forget your mistakes: when someone says to you, *"I can't believe you drew that!,"* just say, *"Thank you."*

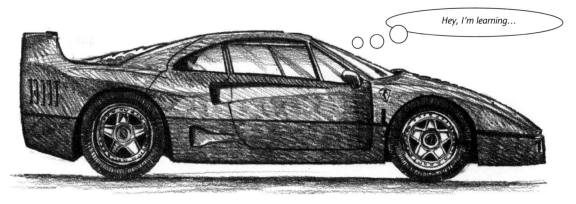

Hey, I'm learning…

FERRARI TESTAROSSA

The more plebian Ferrari is the Testarossa (which means 'red head' in Italian, because the engine's cylinder heads are red, I'm told).

What's distinct about the Testarossa are the lines leading into the air intakes (like the F40 and the Lamborghinis, the engine is behind the driver).

Measure the wheels. Look at these boxes.

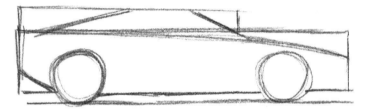

So far, there's nothing too distinctive about the shape of this car. But when you add the lines and the five-part wheels, *voila!* — it's a Testarossa.

PORSCHE 911 TURBO

This car also has its engine in the rear. The 'whale tail' was added to create downward air pressure in the rear at high speeds.

From the top, the back slopes down in one long swoop to the tail lights. Notice how the bumpers stick out in the front and back.

In Germany, where they make these cars, there are stretches of *Autobahn* (freeway) with *no* speed limit. You can be going 100 miles per hour, and one of these little zipsters will pass so fast you can't read the license plate...or get a good photo....

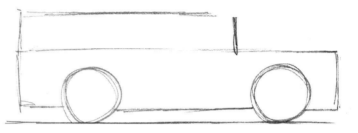

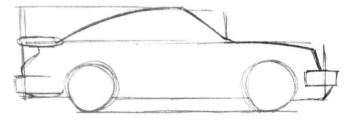

VOLKSWAGEN "BUG"

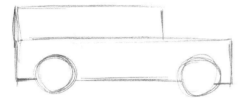

OK, back to earth. This car is a cousin to the Porsche, with its air-cooled engine in the rear. Designed as affordable transportation, it was introduced in America around 1960, and became a hit, largely because of a great advertising campaign.

> *True story:* the author's first car was a aging VW beetle. When he was 15 years old, he paid his parents $50 for it. *It didn't run.* (Smart parents, or what?)

People have done just about everything with Volkswagens: turning them into dune buggies, adding fake Rolls Royce grills on the front. Why not customize yours? Remember, this is *your* drawing! *(How about a satellite dish? A swimming pool? Be creative!)*

VECTOR TWIN TURBO

This is an American high-performance car. The boxes don't help you a whole lot in drawing it — but they do give you straight lines to compare to the curves and angles.

Remember, your job is to observe—compare angles, proportions, figure out how things look. An artist simply looks more carefully than *the average person.*

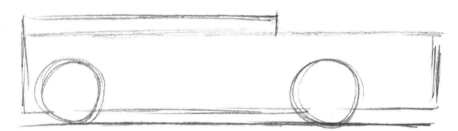

This is an oddly shaped car. Look at how much the front sticks out beyond the wheel—and how little the back does!

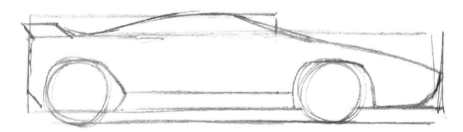

Note the unusual shape of the *wheel wells* and the *window.* Compare the grill of the air intake on the side with the Ferrari Testarossa. Which do you like better?

The Vector Twin Turbo might give you ideas for an imaginary car of your own!

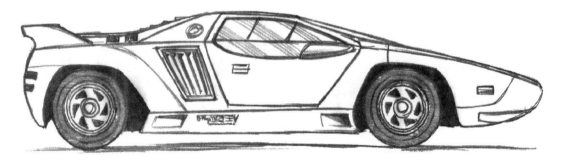

CORVETTE

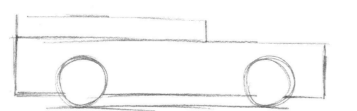

Notice how low the top box is. Measure the wheels!

The Corvette was introduced by Chevrolet in the 1950's, and it has been a favorite ever since! Lots of power, and considerably more affordable than Ferraris, Lamborghinis, or Porsches!

Still, when I took the picture above, I wasn't impressed with the wheels. So, when I made my drawing, I put a different design wheel on the car.

The.front comes up a little, as does the back.

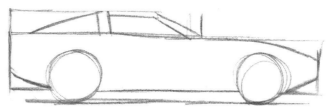

Notice the line along the side!

LOOK!

DODGE VIPER

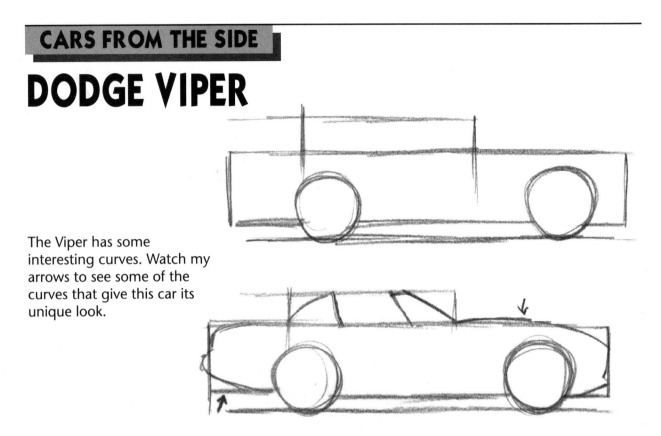

The Viper has some interesting curves. Watch my arrows to see some of the curves that give this car its unique look.

There's a big vent behind the front wheels, sort of like a reverse air scoop. The wheels have a distinctive three-part design.

vent

Note: the exhaust pipes are underneath the doors.

MAZDA RX-7

Just for a little variety, try drawing a car facing the other direction. This car looks very boxy when you start to draw it, so draw your lines lightly! Also, measure carefully, to make sure you get the proportions correct.

Carefully follow the angles and curves you see here...look at how the back is a little higher than the front...

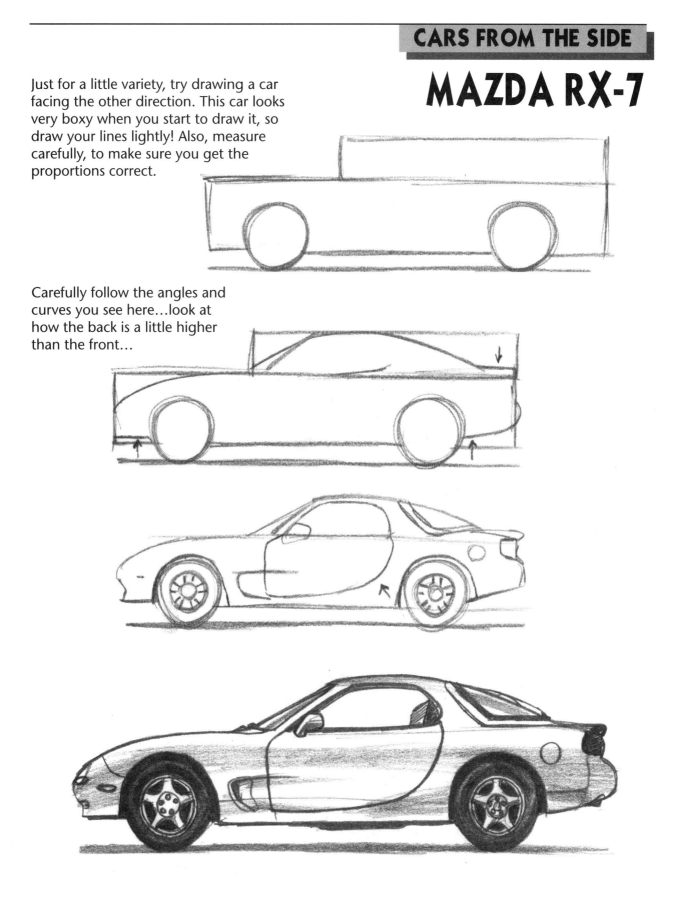

NISSAN 300 ZX TURBO

This car has some very distinctive curves — especially the curve of the back window, which ends in a point. My arrows show you where to look when you draw the curves.

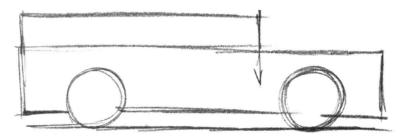

Measure! Measure! Measure!

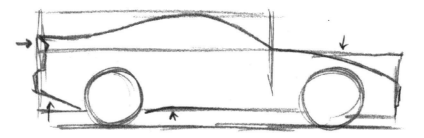

Notice how close the front is to the top of the tire. Also, make sure you draw the back deck of the car higher than the front.

Pay attention to the line down the side, and the unusual rear window design.

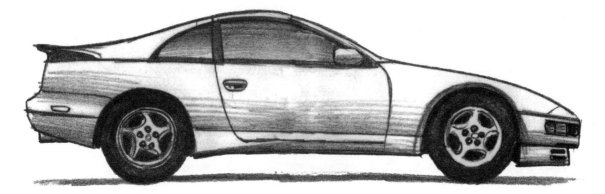

DODGE STEALTH

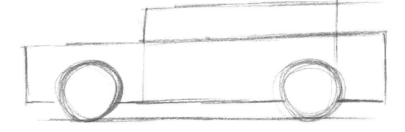

Because the back of the car is higher than the front, it's easiest to draw this if you make the whole bottom box slant forward.

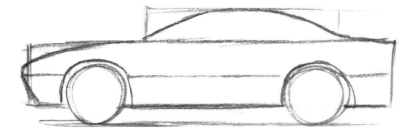

Measure from the wheels. Use the wheels to measure other proportions — the height of the car, how far the front and back stick out past the wheels....

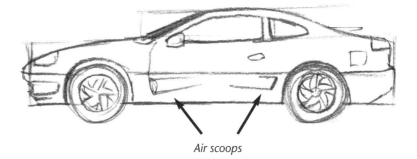

Add the little air scoops on the sides.

Air scoops

MERCEDES 500 SEL

How many wheels…?

This car is designed to carry people in comfort. Unlike sports cars, it has plenty of room, and a back seat.

When you draw a four-door car, it's very important to measure carefully — so that you leave enough room for both doors!

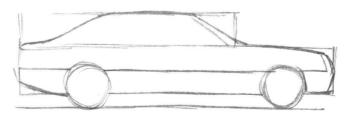

Measure the wheels! Use the wheel measurements to help figure out where to put the lines for the doors. Pay special attention to the headlights and turn signals, and the curve of the passenger compartment above the rear wheel. These details help give this car its distinct look.

Also, notice the distinct way the line of the back door curves.

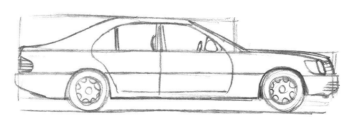

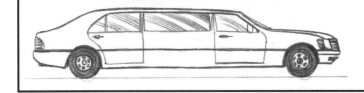

*Looking for a limo?
Why not just stretch a Mercedes?
All I've done is add a section in the middle.*

AUBURN BOATTAIL SPEEDSTER

Some people like the looks of a very elegant older car, but want one with the reliability and performance of modern parts. That's what this replica of a 1930's car gives them.

To draw it, first measure the wheels! Look at the way the hood sticks up above the bottom box — where does the front of the hood stop? *(Clue: look at the front wheel.)*

Which way do the doors open? *(Where's the door handle? Where are the hinges?)*

Notice the wide white walls on the tires — for a period of time, this look was very popular.

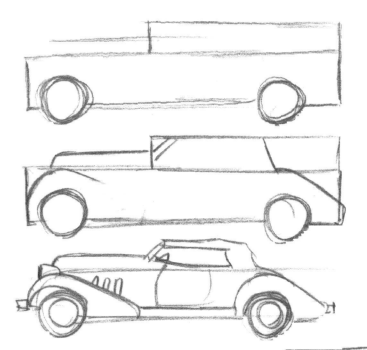

1959 CADILLAC

No, it's not the Batmobile. And no, you don't want to stand behind this car when it's backing up!

Measure from the wheels. Notice how far the back sticks out beyond the rear wheel.

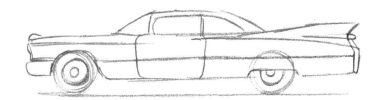

Also, notice how the back of the car curves down, which makes the fins even higher. Measure the tallest part of the tail fin — it's as tall as the side window!

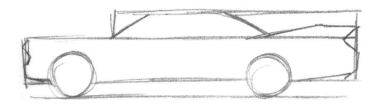

This car is most impressive when you view it from an angle that allows you to see both tail fins. You'll want to understand a little bit about perspective before you try to draw the car from this angle.

1956 CHEVY

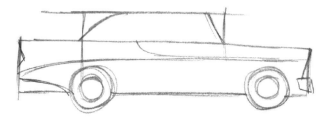

Notice: as with the Cadillac on the opposite page, the line along the side curves down in the back.

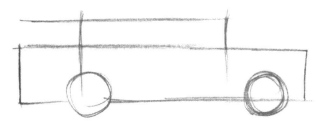

As usual, measure from the wheels. Pay close attention to the height of the two boxes. Also, you can use the wheels to measure where the edges of the door need to be. Because the rear end of this car has been raised, the whole thing slants slightly forward.

Many people enjoy older cars. They either restore them to brand-new condition, or else they customize them, by adding fancy wheels, paint, and other extras.

I left the driver out of my drawing. You can add your own driver.

Add your own smoke, and flames, and whatever else you think the car needs.

1934 FORD MODEL A

Measure the wheels!

How are the boxes different on this car than more modern cars? Where does the front of the bottom box stop? (Measure how high the boxes are, too.)

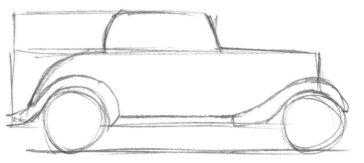

Between the fenders, which stick out to the sides and cover the wheels, is the *running board*—a sort of step to help you get in the car.

On this car, the back, when opened, is a *rumble seat,* so you can ride along in the fresh air.

1905 FRANKLIN

Here's a fun, very old-fashioned car to draw. It's almost as outrageous to look at as a Lamborghini Countache. You could use a car like this to make a fun car for a cartoon.

Measure the wheels. Notice how high the car is. Make sure you include the little lanterns on the sides.

How many spokes do the wheels have?

How fast do you think this car could go?

Answer: not very!

TOYOTA PICKUP

Unlike cars, trucks mainly carry goods instead of people. Light trucks, or pickups, are often used just for people — so I thought you'd enjoy seeing them as well. As always, start by measuring the wheels.

Where does the cab (the part you sit in) end? Measure from the front and back wheels to get the proportions right.

Add lines to show how the fenders flare, or bulge, above the wheels. Add mud flaps to keep rocks and mud from flying in the air behind the tires.

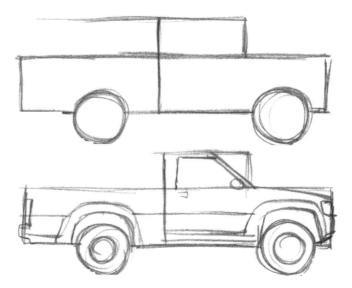

From the side, you can see parts of the exhaust system and drive train underneath.

FORD PICKUP

If you want to draw a large pickup truck, take a look at the photo and measure the wheels. They're smaller, compared to the rest of the truck, than with the smaller pickup.

You may want to add bigger tires. You may want to add custom headers, flames and smoke. You may want to have the front end eight feet in the air. Why not? It's your drawing!

JEEP WRANGLER

The original Jeep was designed for the U.S. military, and served faithfully in the Second World War and various other conflicts. The civilian versions are popular for bouncing around on back roads, and exploring places where there are no roads.

If the person who owns the car in the photo sees this book, he or she will no doubt want to add my lightning bolt design to the side!

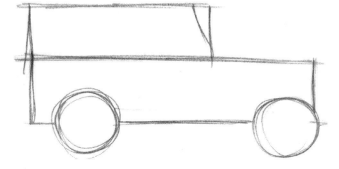

HUMMER

This is the civilian version of the U.S. military's replacement for the venerable Jeep. The military version comes with a variety of options *(add your own machine guns and TOW missiles!).*

The hummer is probably the boxiest vehicle you'll ever see. So stop and really look. With just two boxes and circles, create your own *Hummer.*

Points to notice: where does the bottom of the vehicle line up on the wheels? Where does the front of the vehicle stop (look at the wheel)?

CHEVY ASTRO VAN

A van is not exactly a car, but it's usually used like a car — for transporting people. And it's an easy vehicle to draw!

Pay attention to my arrows as you draw. And remember to start out by measuring the wheels—always try to get the proportions right!

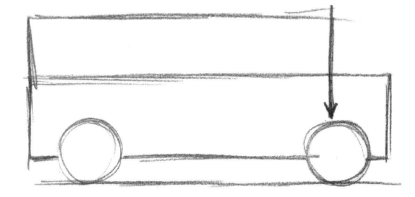

SATURN

This drawing was done from a magazine advertisement—sometimes a great source of *reference material.*

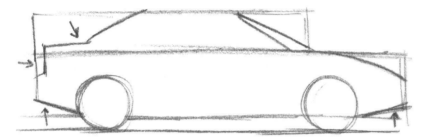

Watch the arrows, and draw the angles carefully.

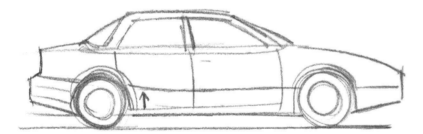

Notice how the line on the side of the Saturn curves slightly upward—this is unusual

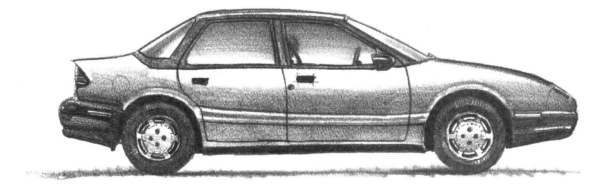

RACING CARS

Top Fuel dragster

When you want to draw racing cars, it's important to remember the system of measuring. Take careful note of how *high* cars are, how *far apart* the wheels are, and the size of the wheels. The boxes you use for regular cars may not work well with some racing cars, so look carefully at your *reference material* and divide the car into boxes that make sense to you.

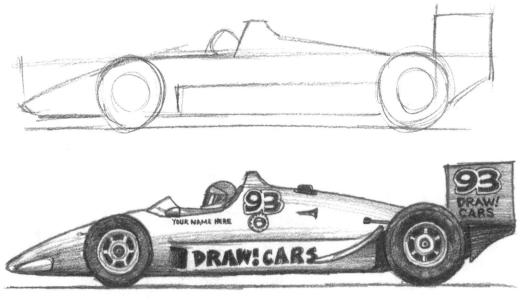

Indy Car

FUN STUFF

Now it's time to have some fun. Let's make up our own, unique, customized cars. You can use the basic circles and boxes to make a rather un-sporty cartoon car, like this one.

How many wheels apart are the front and back wheels?

Or think *fast.* How about a 200-mile-per-hour pickup truck. How do you keep stuff from flying out the back?

Perhaps all you really want is someone else to drive you around in a limo. Let's draw a *fast* limo — the *Lamborrari Limo.* (A rare vehicle, indeed....)

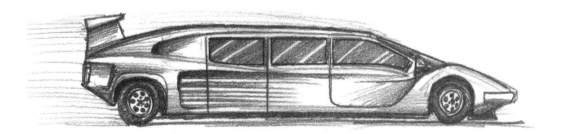

This car looks like I made it up — but actually it's a 1957 Ford Starliner hardtop convertible. Push a button, and the trunk flips up, this huge piece of sheet metal emerges on little legs and sets itself on top of the passenger compartment (and hopefully not the passengers).

Let's make this real car into a made-up car. Perhaps we can…

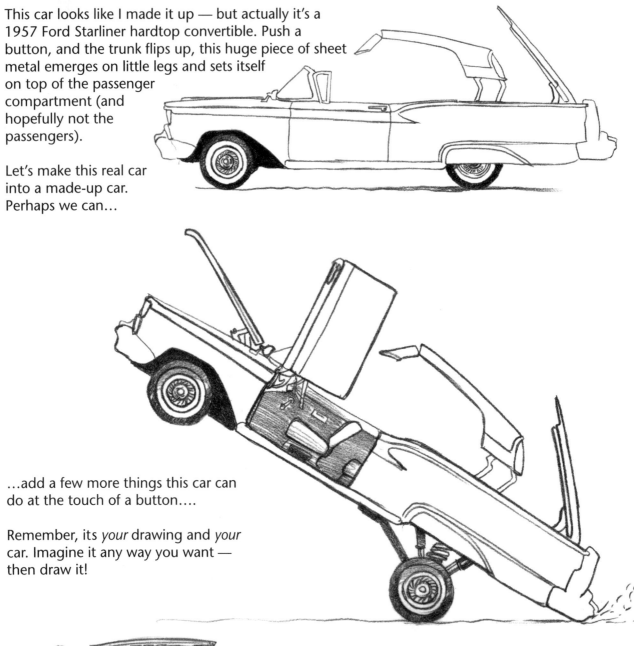

…add a few more things this car can do at the touch of a button….

Remember, its *your* drawing and *your* car. Imagine it any way you want — then draw it!

Do you get tired of riding the same old school bus every day? Use your imagination! Turn that clunky old school bus into a…into a…*whoa, what is that thing, anyway?*

This section deals with drawing cars from different angles. We'll start with boxes and cylinders, and I'll give you some tips for making your drawings more effective. Probably the most important advice is to get good reference material, since drawing cars from an angle is quite a bit more complicated than drawing cars from the side. When you find something in your drawing that doesn't look right, you'll want to be able to compare it to the real thing (or a photo of the real thing).

YES! ◆ You **can!** It's not as easy to draw cars from an angle as it is from the side. I have to be very careful with my own drawings to make everything look right. **The key is practice.** To make a car in 3-D, I recommend you copy from a photo in a magazine advertisement, or any photo you can find. After you've tried drawing from a photo, the explanations that follow will make more sense.

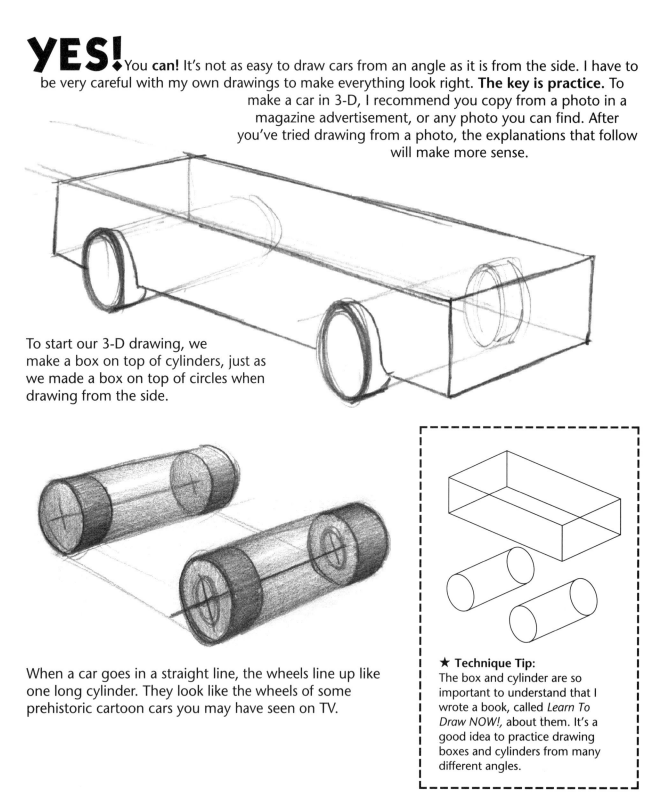

To start our 3-D drawing, we make a box on top of cylinders, just as we made a box on top of circles when drawing from the side.

When a car goes in a straight line, the wheels line up like one long cylinder. They look like the wheels of some prehistoric cartoon cars you may have seen on TV.

★ **Technique Tip:**
The box and cylinder are so important to understand that I wrote a book, called *Learn To Draw NOW!*, about them. It's a good idea to practice drawing boxes and cylinders from many different angles.

When the car turns, however, the front wheels no longer look like one long cylinder. You can see why Fred Flintstone might have trouble steering his prehistoric rig with just one cylinder for his front wheel!

Luckily, when you draw a car, you usually see only two wheels at a time — so you don't have to worry about making a drawing as complicated as this one.

Here's what the front wheels look like when they're turning the other direction. I enjoy the challenge of trying to draw just the forms that make up the finished car…and you may too.

But don't worry if this seems too complicated…by carefully following a photo, you'll automatically get the details right.

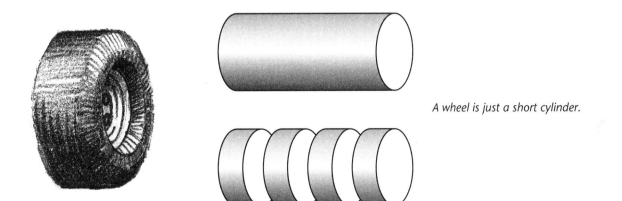

A wheel is just a short cylinder.

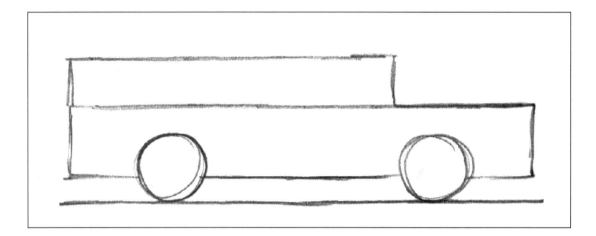

Remember how you added a box on top of the first box when you drew a car from the side? Here's what it looks like in 3-D. The hardest part of this is to *see* how the lines should go — so look carefully at the angle of each of the lines. Which lines in the drawing below are *parallel*?

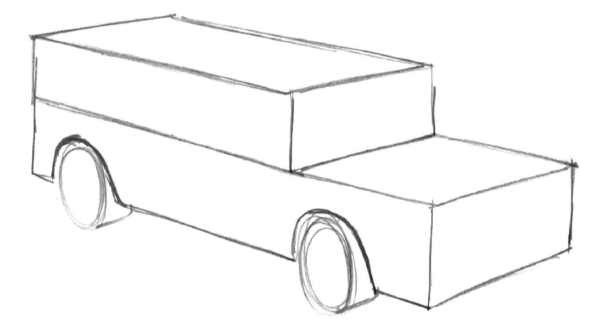

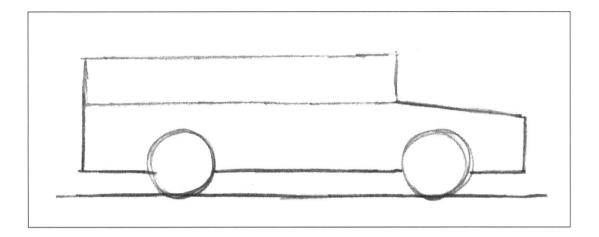

The next step is a fairly easy one — slant the front part of the car downward a little bit.

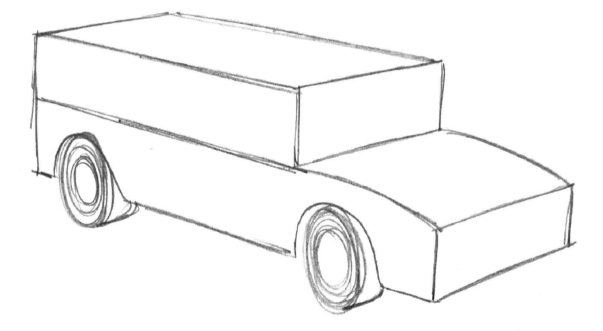

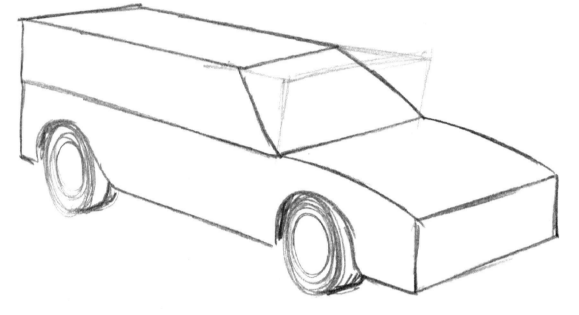

The wind shield also slopes…and here the drawing becomes a little more complicated.

The problem (at least, a problem in terms of drawing) is that the tops of cars are often narrower than the bottoms of cars. In this drawing of a Porsche 959 a, notice how the top part of the car is narrower than the bottom.

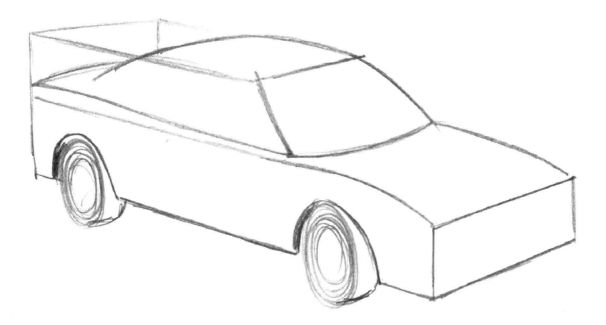

As you take the next steps in turning your boxes into a car, you must watch very carefully — and measure! You can't always trust your eyes alone (see page 58 for some help in measuring angles). Notice how the front of the car isn't square like the box, but rather rounded. Also, notice how the headlights wrap around the side a little bit. It will take practice to get all the details just right. Keep practicing!

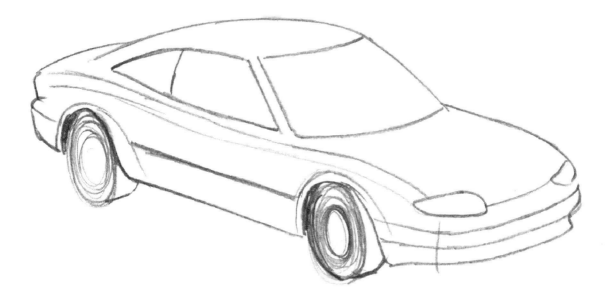

Mazda MX-6 LS

You can finish off the drawing by adding details like wheel designs, rear view mirrors, and door outlines.

Notice how the door outlines curve, revealing the curve of the side of the car. To further convey that curve, I've made my shading lines follow the same contour.

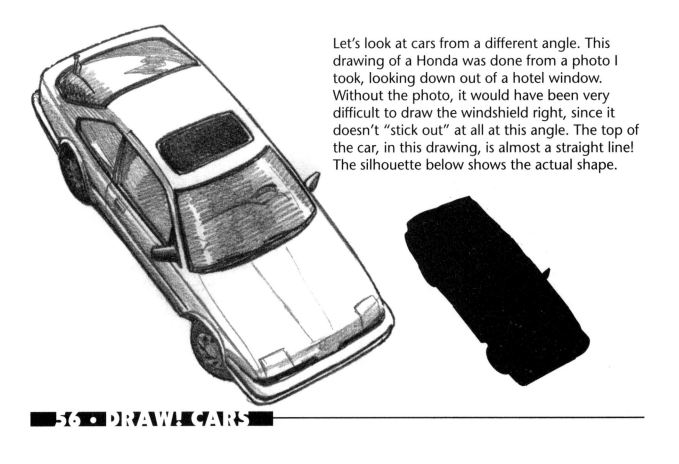

Let's look at cars from a different angle. This drawing of a Honda was done from a photo I took, looking down out of a hotel window. Without the photo, it would have been very difficult to draw the windshield right, since it doesn't "stick out" at all at this angle. The top of the car, in this drawing, is almost a straight line! The silhouette below shows the actual shape.

LOOK!

Ferrari F40

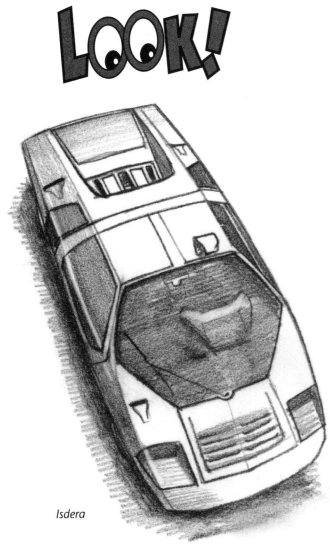

Isdera

The view from above also shows how cars often get narrower at the top. This is what makes some of the exotic cars so difficult to draw. Like a photographer, you have to think about what angle will convey your idea.

The angle of the car on the left reveals its space-age design, but it doesn't look like it's going anywhere. The cars above and below, on the other hand, create a feeling that they're moving towards you.

★ **Technique Tip:** get in the habit of adding shadows. Notice how the Isdera seems to be sitting on the ground, while the Honda on the opposite page looks like it's floating in the air? The shadow makes all the difference.

Lamborghini Countache

★ **Technique Tip:** You still need to measure with your pencil when you draw cars from an angle. Hold it *horizontal* or *vertical* in front of what you're trying to draw. Then compare the angles of the object you see with lines that would be straight across or straight up and down on your paper.

Look at this photo of an Acura (or look at a real car). Now hold your pencil horizontally to help you see the angle you'll need to draw to make the bottom of the car.

To help you see the correct angle to draw for the pillar of the windshield, hold your pencil vertically. On your paper, lay your pencil down horizontally or vertically, and you'll get the angle just right.

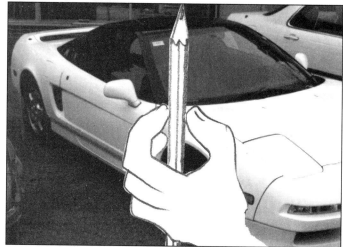

If you're working from a photo or a magazine ad, try this: draw a grid of evenly spaced horizontal and vertical lines on the photo. Then, on another piece of paper, draw the same grid very lightly, and copy parts of the picture block by block. You can also use this technique to make your drawing as big as you want!

***Shortcut:** Use lines on notebook paper for one direction of the grid; then you have to draw lines in one direction only.*

DRAW! CARS

SOME FAVORITES, FROM AN ANGLE

Now use your boxes and cylinders to try drawing some different types of cars from different angles.

Cars drawn from an angle can take several tries. Remember to start out lightly, and be patient. You may have to adjust your drawing before it looks right…don't worry about fixing mistakes as you work—it's simply part of the drawing process!

Learning to see takes time—and practice. Keep looking, comparing, measuring, and fixing.

LAMBORGHINI DIABLO

From this angle, you can start with a box that slopes down toward the front. On this model, the bottom of the side window curves down slightly, as though it's running into the front fender. The rear wheel is wider than the front, so at this angle you don't see the whole wheel design — part of it is hidden.

Diablo front wheel

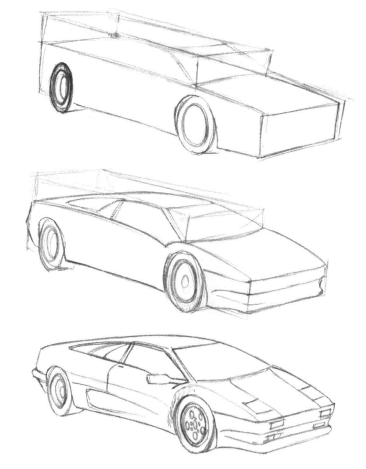

LAMBORGHINI COUNTACHE

The photo at the left is of a Countache, fairly close, taken with a wide-angle lens. Photos of cars are often taken this way for dramatic effect.

On the other hand, sometimes photographers use a telephoto lens, giving a very compressed look. I found this photo on the side of a model kit. I tried drawing it using boxes. You can see the boxes don't help much with such an extreme angle. A grid would have been helpful.

★ **Technique Tip:** measure everything very carefully when drawing a car from this angle — your eyes alone will deceive you!

The rear wheel is wider than the front on many high performance cars.. This is the rear wheel on a Countache.

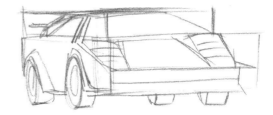

FERRARI F40

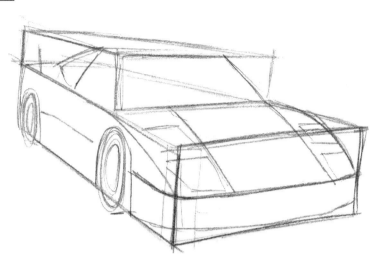

When we drew this Ferrari from the side, I suggested you start with a slanted box for the bottom. Drawing from this front angle, however, the car doesn't appear to slant much towards the front. That's because this drawing is based on a wide-angle photograph, which distorts objects close to the camera.

To keep a drawing like this in proper perspective, it's helpful to lightly draw in lines towards the vanishing points. If you draw the wide-angle distortion well, you'll get a dramatic-looking car. A drawing done without understanding perspective will probably just look distorted.

★ **Technique Tip:** if you don't understand how perspective works, find a book that explains it in easy, step-by-step terms. I was never able to find such a book, so I wrote one: *Learn To Draw 3-D.* It should be available in your library or bookstore.

PORSCHE 911

Here's an actual wide-angle photo, to give you a better idea how perspective works. Because the back corners of the boxes are smaller, the whole thing seems to be zooming towards you. Notice carefully how I've drawn the boxes below.

You have to be extra careful about putting details like headlights in the right place. Draw them very lightly at first, and look to see if they're OK. If not, erase and try again — very lightly.

The rear wheel is much smaller than the front wheel (measure them).

DISTANT COUSINS

The Porsche 959 is a rare, very fast car. It's basically a 911 body with the fenders pushed out and a spoiler added in the rear. In fact, it looks more like an older Porsche, and even a little bit like its relative, the Volkswagen — the drawing below is of the one millionth Volkswagen, built in 1955.

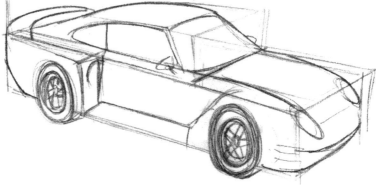

When you draw cars that are mostly round, boxes may seem confusing at first. In fact, they can be very helpful in figuring out angles and curves. The boxes give you something with which to compare the angles and curves in your drawing.

The Volkswagen has small running boards along the sides. The Porsche 959 has something similar in design — but probably not something you'd step on to get into the car!

Porsche 959

1,000,000th VW Beetle (1955)

VECTOR W8

This radical-looking car is the prototype (original model; not yet in production) of the Vector that's to replace the Twin Turbo, which you saw (and drew, I hope) in the first part of this book.

With all the funny little scoops, angles, and modeling, once again the boxes may seem confusing. In fact, the entire car is confusing to draw! If you can start with fairly accurate boxes, you'll have a good start.

If you find a car you really like, try to get your own reference material, preferably including photos from several angles.

Remember the technique of using grids (page 58)? A grid would help you with a car as complex to draw as this one. If you find a photo you can't draw on (as a library book or magazine), see if you can photocopy it — and perhaps enlarge it at the same time.

OLD TIMERS

Old-timer cars can be fun to draw, but they're not easy! Even if you have a good photograph, it might be hard to see details because the earliest cars were often painted black. When these cars were in production, Henry Ford said, "You can have it in any color you want, as long as it's black."

This Model T Ford can be as tricky to draw as any car in this book. If you haven't seen old-timers up close, try to look at photos from as many different angles as possible to get a feel for how they are put together.

If you have a model of one of these, you can sketch directly from it. If you don't have a model, you might have fun building one!

Ford Model T, from around 1920

OLD TIMERS

Old timers have some features you don't often see on newer cars. For example, there are running boards between front and rear fenders. If the fenders bulge out to the sides, then the body of the car needs to be narrower.

Often the engine compartment gets narrower towards the front, and the front may slant backwards slightly, as in this example.

Finally, the front of the car (the grill) ends *between* the front wheels, not in front of them as on a modern car!

British Ford from the 1930's. Notice the mirror on the driver's side, which is the right.

RACING CARS 1

Even more than some of the other cars we've looked at, this type of racing car is made up of fairly basic shapes — cylinders for the wheels and boxes for the body.

This drawing is not any one exact car. If you want to draw an Indy car, try to find your own reference photo, and make your own observations about proportions and details.

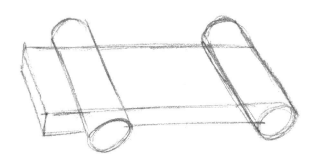

There's a little bit of perspective here — the cylinders for the wheels are closer together, and slightly smaller, at the top.

The box that makes up the body is carved to a point. Imagine carving a block of wood as you draw it.

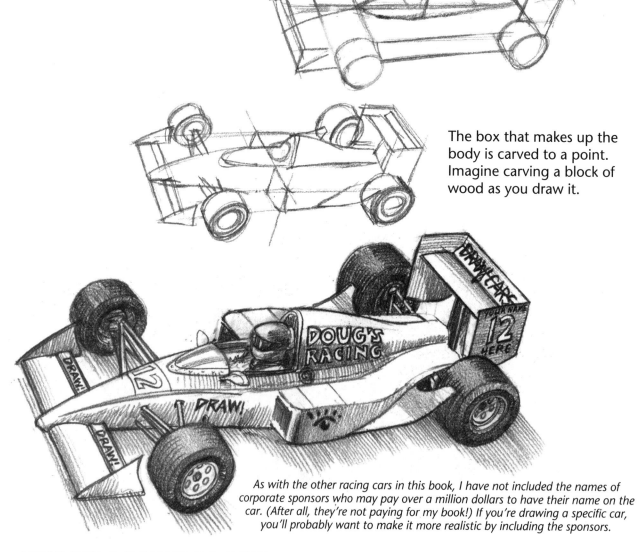

As with the other racing cars in this book, I have not included the names of corporate sponsors who may pay over a million dollars to have their name on the car. (After all, they're not paying for my book!) If you're drawing a specific car, you'll probably want to make it more realistic by including the sponsors.

RACING CARS 2

When you're working from a photo, use the measuring techniques I've shown you at the very start. Work slowly and carefully!

Here's a view of a racing car from a lower angle. once again, it's boxes and cylinders — but you need to look carefully at your reference material, whether my drawing or a photograph, to get the angles of the front right.

★ **Technique tip:** look carefully at the light and dark tones in your reference material. In this drawing, getting the effect of water coming off the front wheel meant carefully erasing part of the rear wheel!

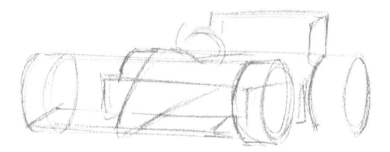

RACING CARS 3

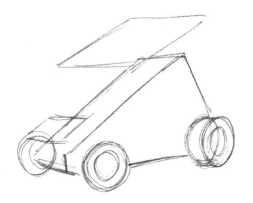

The only thing crazier than the looks of a sprint car is the looks of one tearing around an oval track — at speeds over 80 miles per hour! The driver flings the car into the turns, and the big wings provide air resistance to keep the car from spinning out. Sprint car engines are tuned to deliver 700 horsepower… which is a lot!

RACING CARS 4

There are several classes of drag racing cars, which go from a standing start to well over 200 miles per hour a quarter of a mile later. They're so fast they need parachutes to stop!

This official *Draw! Cars* machine features very large cylinders for rear wheels and radically forward-sloping upper and lower boxes...plus a few other details, which I'm sure you'll add.

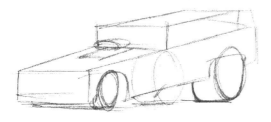

Funny Car

It's important with something this powerful to keep the front wheels on the ground. The front airfoil pushes down. The rear airfoil actually pushes up —can you see why?

Top Fuel Dragster

MONSTER FORD

This page shows you an example of how, as an illustrator, you can use reference material to start, then add your own imagination to create your own picture.

This snapshot, taken with a wide angle lens, shows dramatic perspective, which can make for an exciting drawing. The background of the photo, though, is not very dramatic — so I changed it!

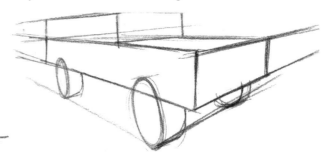

To be sure you're getting the angles right, it helps to understand the basics of perspective. My book *Learn To Draw 3-D* explains perspective in more detail, but you can get the idea from these sketches.

Notice all the little spots, suggesting falling dirt, which help create a sense of action.

DO-IT-YOURSELF MONSTER 1955 FIAT

What can I say? The same year Volkswagen AktienGesellschaft built its one millionth bug, Fiat built this rather mild-looking rig.

Why not use your imagination to turn it into something a bit more formidable...?

LAMBORGHINI — ???

Yes, Lamborghini. Lamborghini doesn't just make exotic cars — in fact, the company started out making tractors. This vehicle was a foray into the go-anywhere-military-vehicle market. Unfortunately, production stopped. Can't you just imagine the U.S. marines intervening to keep some forlorn piece of geography safe for democracy in Lamborghinis?

The front wheels are at different heights as the vehicle makes its way over rough terrain (Notice the lines I've made on the bottoms.)

Compare this with the Hummer. You'll notice it does look somewhat (just *somewhat?*) more stylish than the Hummer.

Notice: part of the trick of making vehicles like this look like they're in motion is positioning them at an angle. Things at an angle tend to look less stable. In the case of off-road vehicles, that definitely adds excitement.

HOW DO YOU DRAW THAT LIKE THAT?

Remember this: it's important to use your imagination, but your imagination is like an engine fueled by facts. The facts, when you're trying to draw real-looking pictures, are real objects or photos of them.

Range Rover. From an ad in a magazine. (You'll find more expensive cars advertised in magazines whose readers tend to have more money. Which makes sense.)

★ **Technique tip:** ask any illustrator who does realistic work if he or she uses photographs. The answer is YES. Maybe a little, maybe a lot; but the simple fact is that to make a drawing that looks like something, you have to know what that something looks like.

Don't say "I copied it from a photo." Say, "Yes, like all professional illustrators, I used reference material."

And they did. Honest.

Prototype (not yet in production) racing car from Mazda, also from an ad, this time in a car magazine. Ads have great photography, and make drivers feel good about driving the type of car that's got such a cool racing version. The author drives a Mazda (COOL, HUH?). It's got 155,000 miles on the odometer. The car isn't quite as exotic as this one, but it does run.

GENUINE IMITATION CAR

Pretty cool-looking car, huh? This is a kit car. I don't know what's underneath it — for all I know, it might be a Corvette. But, like the Auburn Boattail Speedster you saw quite a few pages back, it's an imitation. (In fact, this drawing is based on a photo taken in the same lot outside Sacramento, California.)

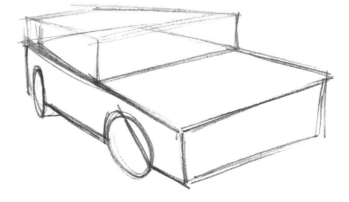

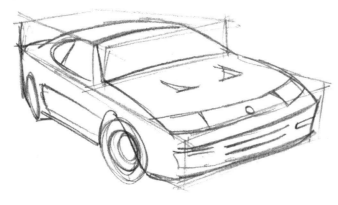

Even if it is sort of a fake, I wouldn't mind cruising in one. Do you think they sell a version that fits onto 10-year-old Mazdas with 155,000 miles on the odometer?

COMING SOON...?

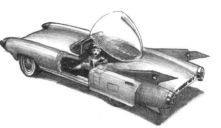

Ethos

Throughout this book, I've been urging you to use your imagination. There's a reason for that. Someday, you might be a designer — your job might be using your imagination to make the best use of facts (wouldn't that be fun?). As we go to press with this book, here are a couple of cars that have shown up recently in auto shows as design concepts. Maybe you'll see them on the street soon. Or maybe — as in the case of the Cadillac Dream Car from the 1950's — not.

Cadillac Dream Car - 1950's

Italdesign's Columbus supervan

GREAT IDEAS 1

Where can you get ideas? Try your library for books on cars, or car magazines. Ads in magazines sometimes have great photos. Even a toy catalog can give you ideas! If all you find is a book with old fuddy-duddy cars, start with them and use your imagination!

After drawing all these fancy cars that other people had designed, I decided I wanted to design my own car. How about a car with two separate sections (and two separate stereos!)? If you had to go somewhere with your parents, they could ride in one section while you rode in the other, listening to different music.

But then, I thought, what if your grandparents wanted to go along too? Wouldn't you need a triple-decker? Who would sit where?

GREAT IDEAS 2

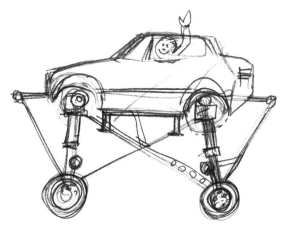

Another idea is to try to solve the problems created by too many cars. The most obvious solution is to have fewer cars, but nobody seems to like that idea! (Least of all, the people who make a living from cars, tires, and petroleum products!)

Here are two possibilities — first, a car that simply lifts itself above the traffic…

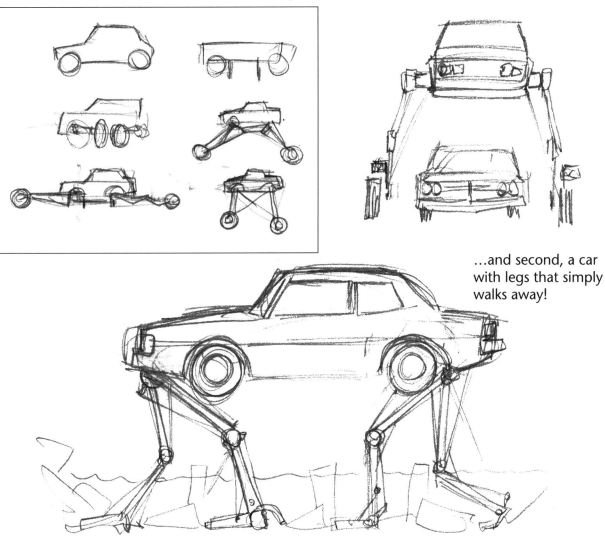

…and second, a car with legs that simply walks away!

USE YOUR IMAGINATION! HAVE FUN!

REMEMBER...

1. Practice

One of the great secrets of our world is that behind every success there's always plenty of practice. The people who do amazing feats of daring, skill, or ingenuity have been practicing, often for much longer than you'd imagine. They've probably failed more often than you can imagine, too—so don't waste your time and energy being discouraged. If your drawings don't look exactly the way you'd like them to, especially when you start out with a new idea, just look more closely, try to figure out what went wrong, and do it again. It *will* be easier (and better) the next time!

2. Save your drawings!

Whenever you do a drawing—or even a sketch—put your initials (or autograph!) and date on it. Save it,, at least for several months. Sometimes, hiding in your portfolio, your drawing will mysteriously improve—! I've seen it happen often with my own drawings, especially the ones I *knew* were no good, but kept anyway....

If you don't have your own portfolio, here's an idea of how you might make one for yourself (you can find a fancy one at an art supply store if you'd rather):

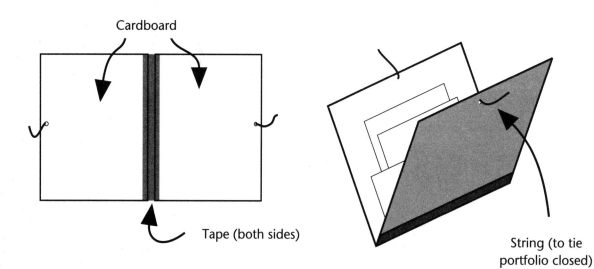

Cardboard

Tape (both sides)

String (to tie portfolio closed)